Still the Animals Enter

Still *the* Animals Enter

Jane Hilberry

Red Hen Press | *Pasadena, CA*

Book layout by Nicole Younce and Selena Trager

Library of Congress Cataloging-in-Publication Data

Names: Hilberry, Jane, author.
Title: Still the animals enter / Jane Hilberry.
Description: First edition. | Pasadena, CA : Red Hen Press, [2016]
Identifiers: LCCN 2015046507 | ISBN 9781597097390 (softcover)
Classification: LCC PS3608.I417 A6 2016 | DDC 811/.6—dc23
LC record available at http://lccn.loc.gov/2015046507

The National Endowment for the Arts, the Los Angeles County Arts Commission, the Los Angeles Department of Cultural Affairs, the Dwight Stuart Youth Fund, the Pasadena Arts & Culture Commission and the City of Pasadena Cultural Affairs Division, the Ahmanson Foundation, and Sony Pictures Entertainment partially support Red Hen Press.

First Edition
Published by Red Hen Press
www.redhen.org

Acknowledgments

The author gratefully acknowledges the publishers of the journals and anthologies in which some of these poems first appeared: *The Burden of the Beholder: Dave Armstrong and the Art of Collage* (The Press at Colorado College, 2010): "Silence"; *The Colorado Independent*: "A Seat for Everyone"; *Columbia Poetry Review*: "For Us" and "To Write My Autobiography"; *Florida Review*: "Binocular Vision"; *Fourteen Hills: The San Francisco State University Review*: "Weightless" and "The Women"; *Hamilton Stone Review*: "We Are Not Made of Sugar"; *The Hudson Review*: "Delayed," "Ours," and "Shadows, Saddle Canyon"; *Lake Effect*: "At the Party" (published as "Mortality at the Party"); *Ohio Edit*: "Reading the Bible at Nine"; *Pinyon Review* : "Childless, She Tends the Garden" and "Her Illness"; *Snakeskin*: "The Bottle Clock"; *String Poet*: "Mere Kissing"; *Tar River Poetry*: "All A's" and "We Were Never Much for Ceremony"; *This Awkward Art: Poems by a Father and Daughter* (Mayapple Press, 2009): "The End Result" and "Tailwind"; *Wingbeats: Exercises and Practice in Poetry*. Ed. Scott Wiggerman and David Meischen (Dos Gatos Press, 2012): "Driving" (published as "My Mother's Clothes").

Many poets—and one mathematician—helped me immensely by reading and commenting on these poems. Thanks to Catherine Barnett, Tony Hoagland, Rachel Feder, Eamon Grennan, Sam Johnston, Rebecca LaRoche, Jim Moore, Kate Northrop, Jonathan Poritz, Diane Seuss, Martha Rhodes and Brian Turner. And, as ever, special thanks to Ellen Bryant Voigt.

Colorado College has generously supported my writing with Benezet, Daehler, and MacLean grants. The Leighton Studios at The Banff Centre provided both solitude and community, and a spectacular setting in which to write. Thanks to Anne Hyde for coordinating a Colorado College manuscript seminar, to my colleagues in the English Department for their friendship, and to Paula Pyne for making life easier in every way.

I am grateful to Kathy Giuffre for reminding me that we don't make art alone, to Karen Sandoval for cups of tea, help in emergencies large and small, and generous friendship, and to Kate Northrop for letting me talk as long as I want to.

To Diane Henn, Kate Holaday, Larry Taylor, and Mary Lou Wild: without you nothing is possible.

This book is for my family:
Adam, Ann, Marilyn, my father Conrad

∞

the memory of my sister Kathy
and the memory of my mother, Marion Hilberry

Tiresome heart, forever living and dying,
House without air, I leave you and lock your door.
Wild swans, come over the town, come over
The town again, trailing your legs and crying!

—*Edna St. Vincent Millay, "Wild Swans"*

Contents

ONE

TWO

THREE

Still the Animals Enter

ONE

This Is Mine

The dead man wants his wife
to be the first to touch his forsaken body,
to lower him from the door where he's hung himself
with a belt.

How lonely to be among the dead!
The ghosts or spirits, if they are that,
don't get to kiss—
the breath bad after a night's sleep,
so one of the lovers, annoyed, says would you *please*
just go brush your teeth—
then the familiar finding of the familiar body—
knee between knees,
bellies touching first, now that they've softened—
the undetectable pull of planets upon one another, gravity
that holds feet to the earth.

It's no longer the *snap!* of magnets,
teenage bodies thrilled at their discovery.
We get to do this?!
A new possession turned over
and over—*I can't believe this is mine!*—
a car the new driver can't quite control—
he turns too wide or too tight—
he looks for the sign and forgets to look at the road—
all scary, all a thrill—

But I'm talking about adults, and a Sunday morning,
and a time in their lives when nothing
seems urgent. I'm talking about the negative space

between them—lamp, candlestick—which melts
with the ordinary heat of habit, two bodies
finding each other, even in sleep—even—
this is the question—in death?

There will be uniforms, sirens, coroners, reporters.
If she touches him, it will be only briefly,
because of the cold.

Weightless,

as children, as if the whole world were a trampoline, each step as much up as down, as if we might escape gravity, might land on rooftops, be seen rising past windows. Though one of us hung over the railing of the tennis court tower and could have fallen, she didn't, and we were bouncing, slow motion, and landing, and rising, slow motion, and landing, our legs tall enough to straddle streets to the candy store, to step over the crossing-guard with her whistle, her sound a wisp underneath us. We could stride to the library, bring books home on our heads, as if they were sugar cubes, or boxes for the tiny glass animals we saved up our allowances to buy at the downtown store where every creature had a fragile wing or leg, where glass ducks glided on mirrored ponds. There were no parents, no such thing as after-dark, twilight lasted, evenings were always. We moved like animals through the neighborhood or like swallows flying over, we didn't live where we lived, we were large, our steps whole blocks, over houses, our bodies light as milkweed seeds. We didn't know what was coming, well, yes we had an inkling, the short hairs in the tub where grownups had showered, we washed them away, we fit together in the bath, splashed water over the edge, we found lakes, larger, where we could swim, our legs reaching into marshes, touching cattails, the murky bottom.

A Hole in the Fence

I wake to the sound of deer prying
the fence with their antlers.

Far north, my woodsy one loves the shuffle

of bears on a trail, unlit
island roads where moose appear, full blown,
in the headlights—

Elsewhere, a woman dances
in the kitchen with her man, a little silliness
before plates are stacked and lights

switched off, before they move
to another room.

Creaking, scraping sounds—
the deer are coming through the fence.

Is your heart lined with fear, like gold leaf?

Outside, how mild the air, lynx
stirring from their dens, birds swelling

with eggs, crocus grunting
out of the bulb.

The trees, leafing, turn

into different creatures, and the wind
makes the tips of the pines gesture—

to me, to one another.

You could be part of this.

The Speeds on the Highway

1. Driving

About to step out of the sleeve of her body,
my mother wants to keep all of her clothes.
She thinks she'll wear the fuchsia shirt again.
She says she wants to start driving. In truth,
she never liked to drive, pushing the wheel
one way or the other in tiny increments.
The speeds on the highway scared her.

2. Delayed

The socks bother her, she must
have them off. The blankets are too
heavy. And me, the size
of a normal human, I want
to be as large as God. Outside,
the clouds drift along, as if
we weren't saying goodbye
for the last time.
They dissolve into fog.
Planes circle but can't
land. Heavens objecting,
I wait three days. Next day,
the sky receives me. I land,
easily, in my sunny state.
I hope the clouds will look in
on my mother. They will know
when it is time to rain.

3. We Were Never Much for Ceremony

As if she'd been launched like an arrow.
We didn't fall to the ground, or rail, or scratch our faces.
We got in the car. We went home for lunch.

Reading the Bible at Nine

When my father asked how far I'd gotten,
I was still in *Genesis*. What I loved
about church was the deep blue of the ceiling

sparked with silver stars. The hymns
would hum me to sleep, or sway me
as I knelt. The wine bit my tongue

and the wafer stuck. What I liked about Jesus
was that he touched lepers, overturned
moneylenders' tables, spoke with Samaritans,

wasn't afraid. I was nine when I asked
to be sprinkled with baptismal water.
Each week after I shed my singing robes,

I would seek, in the low-ceilinged
basement, the doughnut table.
The bite at the center was pure custard.

To Write My Autobiography

I could start with happiness and work backwards
toward a peach tree and three hundred small fruits.

I could inscribe the streetlight's halo, so wide it touched
the magnolia under whose petals we flung

each other into statues. I could introduce you to my sisters.
Marilyn (we call her Marz) likes exclamations:

"Lordy!" Flighty, absent-minded, she liked to stand her head.
Sister Ann can joke or curse in any number of languages.

This story doesn't seem to have a plot, though I've proposed
two characters, at least one setting, and a first-person narrator.

It doesn't move forward like a woman riding a train.
Carrots and apple cores softening in the compost

give me pleasure. The story is imbued with a rich, organic smell.
No plot, but a record played over and over on the wheeling turntable.

"Lord Almighty!" says a sister, "Holy Cow! Thunderation!"
The other sister laughs. Between the tracks,

silence. Needle skimming the vinyl disk. At the end,
if I listen long enough, as the arm scoots

and returns, skids and returns, I might catch a whirr,
a scratch, a whisper of a sister who didn't live.

1956

She sloshes dirty diapers in the toilet, lifts
the lid of the pink plastic bin and leaves them to steep
until washing. Later she lugs the sodden cloths
to the line and clamps each with a clothespin. Silhouettes
of town buildings at dusk, like jigsaw pieces, swell
in the humid air. The diapers have grown large
as sheets. The baby itself is huge as a house.
How did it come out of her, open-mouthed?
The bottles that rattle on the stove, liquid tested
each time on her wrist, are nothing to its hungers.
Too heavy for a stroller. Best to leave it in the crib.
It lies on its back, insect legs moving. The crying
forces her outside, where the air bristles with mosquitoes.
I'll be eaten alive. It is still light, the day impossibly long.

A for Always

1. All A's

My heart learned to sit at its desk
and fold its hands, learned not to scratch
bad words into wood, not to shove
kids at recess. My heart began
to hang its coat on its peg,
to sip milk, slightly warm, through a straw,
to print the answer on the line,
to ascend through reading groups:
Orange, Yellow, Green, Blue.
My heart got all A's.
A for Alone. A for Always.

2. Poem Made of Cold

Streetlight orbs of blowing snow.

(The mother asleep in the heat of the father's body.)

Thumbs numb, nostrils frozen stuck.
Then the sigh of the school bus door's pneumatic hinge.

3. Cooking Show

Lemon zesters, garlic presses, oil of truffle,
handfuls of scallops. The chef knows how
to slice onion, knuckle gauging the blade.

Sizzle, scent of rosemary, sting of citrus.
A woman watches in her kitchen, counters wiped,
the television sound turned off.

4. In a Bar, Watching Bodies Touch

The amphibian evolves so slowly
into reptile that it doesn't notice
the difference between water and air.
Yet the brain stirs at the water's edge:
I'm thirsty, I'm thirsty, I'm thirsty.

In the Yellow House

Sunday night dinner was popcorn, cinnamon toast.
We watched Walt Disney's *Wonderful World of Color*
on the black and white TV.

At seven, I believed we could all learn Esperanto.
I lay on my stomach to study
the bright books my mother brought home.

My mother loved words, Latin derivations,
strict configurations of grammar.
She must have known how histories cling, odd clusters
of consonants, silent letters, mystifying idioms.

Once, one of my cousins, visiting,
spoke a name, asked a question we knew better
than to ask. I climbed over the couch to listen.

The Middle East erupted in war. The concrete floors
in the house made my mother's legs ache.
I lay on my stomach, preparing.

A Seat for Everyone

—for Rick Perry

And you were never a child, correct?
You never missed your father when he was on a business trip.
You walked home from school alone and maybe you were so safe you didn't even think
of safety, or maybe you were a little afraid, am I right, about the bigger boy,
who might call you names as you walked past his house? Or were you never a child?
Send them home!
Or maybe you had a mother who would have packed your lunchbox
and put you on a yellow school bus to another country, with strangers,
knowing she might not see you again. Your mother would have done that, right?
Because the world is safe for children. Or because you were never a child.
If your father didn't come home one night (no body in the rosebushes,
nothing gruesome, but say he disappeared), well, things happen.
Not every child has the luxury of a father. Or brothers.
And when you walk back into that place you call childhood,
if you had a childhood, is that the place you send these children
when you send them home? Maybe so. Maybe you send them
to a house with brick walls and a fireplace, to mother waking them for school
at the same hour every morning and dinner at six hot in the serving dishes,
the table set, a seat for everyone. Maybe you *were* a child.
Maybe you think you were every child.

Binocular Vision

The eye doctor can't stop staring
at the photo of Marie and her sisters,

their eyes all wandering, crossed, turned in.
They're the ones who survived,

the other siblings brain-damaged, or dead.
Resting her forehead in the black cradle

of the doctor's machine, Marie sees a cage
on one side, a bird on the other.

He wants her eyes to work together
to bring the bird inside the cage.

Does she want to see?
Infant in a crib.

Mother's steps approaching.

The Bottle Clock

No and *not-time-yet.*
The crying a *doesn't-*
matter, a *mother-knows-*
best, a book, a doctor.
The bottles, glass, bounce
in boiling water, nipples
dry on a dishcloth.

Tailwind

At the pool he finds fins his size
in a big blue bin and works
his feet into the rubbery slots.
After a year, he's decided to return
to his mother. He sinks
through turquoise water,
tries to walk on the bottom.
Then he asks me to lift
his feet and lodge the flippers
on the pool's rim while he stretches
on his belly to get a start.
It's awkward. I don't see
how it can work. He pushes off,
gets the feel of the fins and,
like an airplane with tailwind,
speeds the across the blue.

Order

Each object touched, housed, like a child put to bed
with stories and backrubs. The kitchen still.
No mice about the sink. Hands sort silver:
the bishop's palm anointing heads, lines of girls in white,
communicants at the altar, the rector's wife, who had polio,
holding the rail, lowering herself to kneel—then the bread,
then the wine. Although no one believed Jesus would rise again,

he did—*that* was a surprise, but we mark it with ritual:
palm strands that splinter the fingers, cross towering
down the aisle on an acolyte-borne pole, shrouded in black.
At home after dinner, when other people's children play
till parents' voices thread them home, one can dry the dishes
and stack them in a way that pleases, one can offer this kindness,
this duty, this reverence to the gods of evening. The gods of solitude.

The gods of coming sleep, in which dreams do whatever they please.

The Game

Mr. Smith made a loaf of French bread every day for a year,
studying the chemistry of yeast and sugar, perfecting
the kneading of air into dough, until he could produce
the loaf he wanted, every time. Needless to say, he was
a mathematician. If you walked by his house, you might hear
his concertina, the complex breathing of the fabric pleats
and the song like a human voice made by pressing buttons.

When I was ten and couldn't do my math problems,
my father took me to the Smith's house, where I sat
on the floor at the round coffee table, my fifth grade
textbook open to the homework, and Mr. Smith showed me
how fractions worked. It was like calling upon Jesus
to heal a sprained thumb.
                         When I see him now,
he still asks about the game, with that look
of curiosity, an intelligence that doesn't miss a detail
or nuance. "And one of the rules," he says, with a laugh
quick and rilled as an old tune, "one of the rules
was that you could cheat?" *Three Steps to Germany*
we called it. We must have inherited it, but from whom?

"Three Steps to Germany!" the IT shouted,
and the rest yelled back, "EXTRA STEP!"
We dashed toward the starting line to take four
of our legs' largest steps. Then the cheating began:
if the IT wasn't looking, you could inch toward the finish line, or take
a big stride. But if the IT saw you move, you were fair game,
to be chased, to be tagged. And Mr. Smith, who never missed
a note in an arpeggio, never guessed at the amount of sugar or yeast—
well, maybe he longed back to the childhood he might have had
in which dusk was just the temperature of water on a wrist.

Outside

Summer's cricket has long stopped chirping,
no lamp to carry through the winter.

Heavy dump truck in the predawn slush,
the sleeping street, and the children ask,

Who will hold me now?

No More

No more need to slug out of bed in the morning, to lean on coffee and sugar,
or simply to stay in the curtained room while his family traces its circles,
front door, side door, oven door, microwave, refrigerator door, sliding door

to the patio and the voices as strange as lemonade. No more need to buckle
children into car seats, to spray spot remover on the clothes, the rug. No need
to polish shoes, no need for dry cleaning, tickets, car wax, tire spray, oil changes,

post office box, bills returned in envelopes with the address showing properly
through the cellophane window. No more lawns and rocks and fountains,
sump pumps, gardens and spades and seeds and the ensuing fruits.

The dishes needed to be done by hand, not in the dishwasher:
his wife's single absolute. All else, stripped back, came down to love.
Blood presses on the brain stem, the liver tired of its functions.

The skin tired of being pink. A body in a bed, unconscious, hearing
or not hearing. And she whose promise was unbending, says,
"I didn't know how to do different."
                              What am I saying? That I envy

the man in a coma on the hospital bed? Close-eyed, mute, he transmits
the way bats send radar, or ships in fog. His children come bedside.
I could stop—scrubbing my sink, plucking moths from windowsills,

kneeling to sweep lint from beneath the bed.
He grew pink roses. Standing in his front yard, the screen
door propped open, he told me how to use the petals to make potpourri.

Wormhole

The mice have been leaving their love notes
under the sink, the bed. Craig the exterminator says
they don't see well so they run along the baseboards,
navigating by their whiskers. I've covered the gap
in the cupboard floor with *David Copperfield*.
Craig moves the volume to drop bait, then replaces it.
Is it a good story? he asks.

                                                Just outside, a buck languishes,
an open pink wound, a big mound of abscess
exposed on his belly.

Craig stops the holes under the sink with steel wool,
but still the animals enter:
a pair of tigers loose in the family room
bears scavenging on the railroad tracks
a lion fine as a *Dürer* etched between stars
on the dark blue background of sleep.

We Are Not Made of Sugar

Not afraid of the cold. Other fears:
manila folders, narrow windows.

⁓

A pumpkin in the garden softens. In spring
a forest of tiny stalks,

translucent, breakable, each bearing its tiny
two-leaved flag. *Victory*, it says, and *surrender*.

⁓

If we can't dance in flame and sleep on sheets
of ash, our love is not immortal.

⁓

Wir sind doch nicht aus Zucker,
the German woman says, striding into the rain.

But we are: sugar on each others' tongues.

TWO

Very lovely, don't pick it up

A woman and her lover make appointments
to talk, though neither is required to say what—
or to say more than—

a man builds a house and lives only on the perimeter,
picks only what grows by the fence

*Truly, I do, though I might not
be able—*

Here at my table, the leaves of the poinsettias
suddenly look like fabric or skin—

*Leave me alone,
leave me alone, leave me alone*

Washing the windows, not going inside

Something I'd like to lie down in, those
poinsettia quilts

Possibly, this time

A hole in the fence where the deer,
sensing something better on the other side—
apples sagging on branches—break through,
their antlers scraping the wood slats,
and file in, elegant, decorous,
placing their hooves on the grass
as if they were weighty objects,

and the ticks from the deer
bed in the long grass until one is swept
into the cushy fur of the golden retriever
who romps and gallops
turns tight circles in the yard
who loves above all
his owner
bounds back
to her shoves her legs
rubs himself against her ankles
pale in summer beneath the spiky aspens
gives her the tick, a kiss.

And like a radio broadcast which starts
behind glass but beams its signal
into kitchens across the city,
the state, into car radios
as men drive away from home
(possibly, this time, not coming back),
into offices where fluorescence
makes the workers look ill, sends its song
into the night when most lights

are quenched, except
a slow string as the janitor makes his way
down the hall, radio hooked
to the edge of his cleaning cart—

so the bite, unremarked,
sends its shock waves, broadcasts itself
to all of us in the precise locations
where we hear the news
(her head in a bag
she herself taped shut, then waited
for the air to run out—)

each point on the map a pin fixed to a red thread
that stretches to her house, her couch—
our threads crossing threads stretched
to other pins (cocktail of drugs,
blood filling the bath)—

we're all bound now

aghast and grieved at the hole they opened up
tore by force
to make their way to another world.

the sky watched

the clouds seating and reseating themselves

treetops shifting side to side

the roads balling into a fist around her house

the clouds unable to sit still

and the deer, normally calm, clattered and shoved
their way through the fence

to pose, one stag statue-like, still except
for a twitch on the long torso
and a head swiveling to face the plate glass

if we had known, if only

Rowboat on a Lake of Words

One thing is for sure, the oars are useless now, or lost—

she didn't give, he criticized, the children didn't eat, the father
read his science books, he never said I love, *it was a remarkable*
moment, time stood still, I am chopping the ends off the green beans,
my feet hurt, can I return these shoes? Could I possibly
get a glass of milk?
                                And now the words
could be anything, minnows, mica, diamonds,
the chain mail a boy forges with his pliers,
sitting through German class. Some fine
embroidery. A mirror. Silver mesh.

—after May Stevens

New Life

—Colorado Springs

The silence became difficult so we
forsook silence.

We ate images to fill up. Music,
reassuring rock, hands in the air,

hand in the air, arm extended,
palm forward. An invitation, a shield.

The steel beams above our heads
held us in place below. We swayed,

we shifted. We were fine here,
not desperate. Something flowed into

our open mouths. We opened our hearts.
There was nothing in sight, no cross.

One or two crosses
and a stage-managed light.

This was all we needed, and we needed
what a man spoke as he paced

and paused and paced and turned
and faced us and gave us words.

A wafer small as a chiclet
a thimble of wine.

We were assured we'd never leave
though the exits were marked:

north, northwest, southwest, southeast
as in a stadium.

❧

Outside the air, as always, is crisply
blue or warmly blue, the sky.

The pines grow from stone,
no soil apparent. A wind pushes

a wind pushes their tops.

Window

I loved a man who hated luxury and—full turn—loved a man
who relished it. Between them a window; they touch hands
through the pane. As if in an etching, monochrome.
Both were solicitous. The fabric on one's bed was wool,
ponderous, a cool wind basting us while we slept.
The second one's pulse ran fast; he moved too swiftly to name
what stirred inside. Oh no, I have not stopped loving either—
though I am in exile, watching these men, together, from a distance.

Childless, She Tends the Garden

Half inch deep, rows two feet apart. The ground
grows plump with rain. The moon casts its eye

and closes its eye, and the sun draws them up:
a sprout splits each seed's white sides.

Bananas rot to softness in the compost heap.
Cut grass, raked leaves. Beetles shelter

under eggshells. Seedlings drink
from the shoveled mulch. Each finds its way

to stand and spread, or vine toward the gate,
while marigolds blare their protective scents.

Squirrels, perched on fence slats, wait
for sunflowers to sag within reach. Meanwhile,

the lupine breed and regress, purple giving way
to pastel, a spray of white. Pumpkins

soften and cave. The chard grows long into fall.
Many things need tending. I pick up the rake.

Her Illness

The road itself is hell,
all lived delight a lack.
The road is tenderness.
Lichen embraces stone.
A strange November sleep.
Somber knowledge: God
is an inward root
gradual, spindly, deep.

—after Roethke

The End Result

At times in her sickness, her eyes,
fixed on me, became opaque,
and I expected her to speak
something terrible in its import.

At other times my mother was softer
than she'd ever been. I would lie in bed
beside her, something I had never done.
She said, *I have the best daughters*

anyone could have. I saw my opening:
I haven't always been a good one.
After the smallest pause, she said,
I'm pleased with the end result.

It wasn't funny except in that quiet way
she had with words, a humor I didn't recognize
until it became prominent
as the bones in her chest, her cheeks.

Pleased with the end result.
There was no better architect of diction.
She said it precisely, her language
elevated enough to clear the top

of my wrongs: my barely concealed
contempt, my towering silences.
On her flight out of the world,
she knew just how to judge.

Young Women on Apartment Lawn

One in a pink bathrobe, the other in blue. One holds closed
her robe; the other tugs a leashed dog. A man approaches,
black jacket, grey hair. They talk, they laugh,
the women touch his arm. Behind them the mountain sports
a light coat of snow. Clouds swirl the peak in a white bouffant.
Now their laughter bounces in the concrete stairwell.
From where I sit, I see sparrows flitter and flock, landing,
but not staying more than an instant on any branch.

Descent

After three years perched
in my bird's nest home,
where I've watched
mountains unfold their softnesses,
velvety pine and rusted cottonwoods
below the slate faces of the peaks,
where I've watched
clouds sink and settle
sexually into the valleys—
after years of celibacy
and solitude,
today I descend
three flights of stairs,
with men to cart furniture,
books in my arms. I pass
the doors of neighbors I didn't know
and ones I didn't like
(the woman who had conversations with her dog
as if he could understand and I could not:
"Come here, Fluffy. Not everyone likes dogs
as much as we do").
                    I'm descending
like Antaeus to earth again,
to feel damp grass, to live among trees.

❦

At my friend's memorial, after the service,
women gathered in the bathroom. One said,

"What about the men? Someone
should have spoken about the men."

❧

We released doves, twelve of them, out of a crate.
My dove, white, turned its head side to side sharply.
I talked to it the way I would to soothe a child.
My friend killed herself just after Christmas.

❧

The book says: buy matching nightstands, an extra toothbrush.
Clear some closet space. The lover will appear.

Yesterday I saw a doctor lift a sheet to reveal
two human hearts.
One was compact, neat in the doctor's palm.
The second was huge, loose, a worn-out
towel in a rag heap, spongy,
as if, tossed in water, it would grow
still larger.

❧

My mother had many suitors, several fiancés,
one husband. To me, she'd say,
"What about Paul? Paul seems like a nice boy."
I rejected marriage, the institution, the dress, the ring,
the ceremony, the sharing a bed every night for the rest of one's life,

the crunching of cereal at the breakfast table,
the children, grandchildren.

The doves flew—the tan one, the leader,
released first, then the other eleven, all white,
off the balcony, in air still wet with rain
against a blue sky, perfect conditions
for a rainbow. We lifted the birds
and tossed them lightly
to launch them,
although they didn't need our help.

My friend didn't die of loneliness.
She was not reluctant to date,
to sleep with men she liked.
But the slow erosion
of her brain, not to think clearly—

I am coming down from my observation deck, the balcony
where I watched the mountains' changing tableaux—
arrangements of rock and cloud and snow.

A man I know, opposed to marriage, dissuaded many couples
from being wed. Married himself now, happily,
he still doesn't believe in it, he says.

He's just given up on being right.

⚜

Ponderosa pine, blue spruce, juniper, leafing lilac:
from my ground floor windows, I can't see

past the green. Boxes rest on the floorboards.
Each cup and plate must be unwrapped,

washed, placed on a shelf, in a cupboard.
The walls want the touch of a roller or brush,

but I won't wait to hang the first painting:
a woman holds a dove to her chest.

The bird's neck fills the space between her breasts.

The Dead

The dead get angry if they're kept
    on a tether

They want freedom, release
    from *shouldn't have*

They like to float on their backs, ears full
    of the dulling surge

The loft and slough reminds them
    what time was like

When they open their eyes
    they can see us,

like carp, our mouths moving—
    No matter how

we shout at them
    they don't hear

THREE

Mere Kissing

He rose when touched, a denser appetite.
He saw all things are made of skin and stone
and dreamed a creature tinged with beast.

I'd grown alone in darling inwardness,
my stillness rooted in the golden mean—
but the solemn may grow ravenous.

Song and moon and throat became our need.
Mere kissing was the substance of our thought.
We shook dry blossoms, loosening their seed.

—after Roethke

For Us

Brush dipped, you touched the tip
to the paper—it might have been the smooth
of my stomach, and I did—I led you

to the bed. You were natural, opening
like a flower, your penis, freesia,
the light scent. You didn't need to be taught.

In dreams, I play kick the can with boys
from elementary school—
The sky is purple. The crickets thrill. For us,

it was easy as a river's twisting. My hunger—
red tongues, orange flames, a flicker
of blue. You wore yourself lightly,

dirty jeans, button fly, work shirt.

Ours

Each step stitches them together
as they walk the dog, each breath at night
winds them, together, into sleep's cocoon.
Even the fights, sharpening
the blades of anger and accusation:
knives side by side
in a drawer. Her clumsiness
so familiar he knows when to reach
beneath the bowl she lifts.

                            When he sees me,
he says a word that meant something to us,
the name of a planet. We camped by a lake
and read out loud until it was too dark to see.
It was already over then, the sky
borrowing its color from the fire,
then both out.
Still I wanted his hand, to wind his fingers
into mine.

                 At night he and his wife lock the doors,
extinguish the lights and turn to each other.
I am a conversation never had.

                           We had a time
that was ours. He held my new kitten
inside his shirt. We threaded roads to mining towns
in his truck. When he touched me,
I couldn't believe—

I couldn't believe my luck.

The Women

They're both Midwestern, awed by the gold
of Colorado sun. He never suspects

they meet, compare his gifts—none, thank God, alike—
praise his manners, always the gentleman,

taking the street side when they walk. The older one
is a better cook, better gardener. It's right

that she should live with him. They work this out
at the glass table, bare feet burrowed in the fur

of his beloved dog. My God! one thinks, I see
how he fell in love with her. The poppies nod.

The glasses of iced tea begin to sweat.

Measures

Words stitched in perfect rows. I know
the end of the book, but can't stop reading.

The most of anger I can muster is a minor third.
You are perfect fourths. This is no garment,

this shift I wear in secret. Give me a gown
made with the sweep of a wand.

Give me a song that's not in measures.

Geometry, Complicated

I dreamed of a lover from years ago,
and a black granite floor with markings
to direct me in my solo dance,
for which I was not prepared. A tall man,
my lover stood behind me and curled his arms
around my shoulders to reassure.
And what the dream gave back
was not so much the depth of aftershave,
the Randy Travis voice I felt moving
in his chest—not so much that
as a specific geometry:

my lover's arms an arch,
as you'd see in a cathedral or ballroom—
or a greenhouse fashioned from bowed wood,
or the bent sky over the raft where we lay
watching dust disintegrate in the Perseids.
I'm not talking about sex, but architecture,
and I mean that unlike the dream,
which is already fading, unlike
the love affair, which lasted only months,
this shape remains, a place
where for a time he sheltered me.

❧

I imagine my sister reading this poem and saying, What?!!! What?! Have
you forgotten? He slept with you at camp and didn't walk you back, and you
got lost in the woods! Did you forget that?!

Yes, I say, I know I know. But poetry is about imagination, and that space
I described is real—it's something inside of me—

Sister: So you can make up whatever you want, and make it sound all
nostalgic and romantic?

Me, tentative:—Poetic license?

Sister: Poetic bullshit!

∽

This week at my sister's house, it took nine attempts,
involving two whole pies (one pumpkin, one cherry)
to help her son, my nephew, make a four-second
stop animation film. When I asked my nephew a question
and he said, "I don't care," I yelled at him for being rude.

We decided to clean the house, stuffing worn-out clothes
and shoes and papers and toys into garbage bags.
Luckily we laughed as we hauled the plastic bags back
from the freezing driveway at midnight to sort through the trash
in case we had thrown out the Christmas cash, which was missing.

My sister and nephew and I love to swim, to bodysurf
on a windy day in Lake Michigan, slogging through water
until we catch a wave strong enough to shoot us toward shore,
and even then, it's pebbles in the face as the wave grinds us
into the shallows and sand in our suits for hours afterwards,
in our ears and hair for days.

Dishes and more dishes. Laundry in heaps
fills the basement. I yelled at my nephew.
I am afraid I will estrange myself from him
over stupid things. Later in the day,
he comes up behind me at the kitchen sink
and hugs me with his newfound football strength.
He says, "We're all crabby today."

My friend Kathy says, "I never count on my virtues.
My vices are much more reliable."

Our planned glamorous vacations always fail:
we invite the neighbor boy, who's having a breakdown,
or we've made a horrible choice about that hotel
we booked online.

But no, we didn't throw the money away.
It was tucked in an envelope, inside a book.

At the Party

He goes by Mort. He pretends not to know much, lets us all believe that he's less evolved than we are, a Caliban. Only the kindest among us tries to make conversation with him. He doesn't nod or laugh or recall that time when the same thing happened to him. He's like an oversized child up past its bedtime. Like the St. Bernard who mostly lies on the floor and yawns, but occasionally stands and shakes the brass bell on its collar. Most of us avoid him. The doctors in the room could learn something from him: he knows how the nerves are laced and knotted, how the perineum tears when a new one comes into the world, how viruses reside in saliva, passing happily from tongue to tongue. But even they are afraid of his strangeness, his immunity to social graces. Has he ever loved anyone? No one bothers to speculate. He doesn't hold a grudge, even though we shun him, even though conversation moves around him all evening like currents around a rock, even though no one touches him, not a handshake or a brush against the elbow, even though no one laughingly wipes a little mustard from the corner of his mouth. He doesn't resent us. He memorizes eye colors, the jokes we repeat at every chance, the textures of our skin. The kinds of shoes we wear. The curl of our ears. He doesn't whisper, has no need to seduce. Only he will sleep with each of us.

Silence

*Now the Sirens have a still more fatal weapon than
their song, namely their silence.*
—Franz Kafka

all the spaces between the notes of birds' songs,
all the bodies so deep in rest
they forget the day's rocking on the boat,
all the longing looks that go wordless

silence of insects, in the trough of their buzzing
silence within numbers, the loops of the 6 and the 9
silence of a woman's thigh

silence of schist a billion years old. Sex requires sound—
quick punctuated cries and slow outlettings of breath—

but the silence before

silence of glass

A Map of Calgary

At night after you're asleep, I study the map
of your city. In my mind, Fourth Street runs parallel
to the river, but on the page it is perpendicular. Your house
backs to the West, but I would follow the highway
in front to find mountains. Someone must have figured out
when to speak, when to be quiet, when to notice,
when to overlook, how to find the lake of love,
over and over, in one's chest. The house
is small. I can master it: my towel
on the left, yours on the right.
Dish rack, tea bags, cupboards, knives, cloth napkins.

You'd do away with maps and follow trails,
cedar waxwings, apples still holding to the branch
after winter. You grew up on skis, in snow, on ice.
My childhood was a tree house, each plank painted
from a leftover basement can. I threw pebbles
at Kelly's window to tell her to come outside.
We knew where the spinster sisters lived,
which houses had dogs, which grownups would yell
if we cut through their yards.

On your couch tonight, we looked at photos of harbor seals.
I know you recall their smell, their grunts, tangles
of kelp, the salt wind that touched your cheeks
more times than I can match in all days from now on.

We found each other late.
I can't take you back to stand under Kelly's window.

I can't see seals or the blues of glacial ice.
Across your street, they are building an old folks' home.
By the time they finish, you say, you'll be ready to move in.
Where will I be? Girder by girder, the building rises.

Night Swimming

We can hardly
make them out, the children,

swept
to a crest, dropped, pulled away
toward horizon

then lifted, the children,

as if in the palm of a huge hand, a dozen feet
to the top of a curl,

dropped.
Don't call their names.

No shore is safe:

let them rejoice
tonight

in the large and chilly waters—

I never liked dogs.

This one romps, rubs, circles
the man's pale ankles.

The daughter in his arms leans sideways
to touch her head against his head.

She's excited to give her mother the flowers
she wrenched from their stems.

Leave the door open.
The dog wants in—

Open a door so a dog
can come twisting barreling in

heedless oh heedless nudging
into crotches rubbing legs

his owner an itch

Have you ever, says the man,
seen so much life in a creature?

so the pots in the kitchen rattle   so the floors touch our feet

so my dreams migrate to you during the night   yours to me
we drink them in the morning   black and hot
we invented this life of sheet music   the tips of pens
grocery lists painted in oils   we make
no promises   if the night winds us up like a German clock
we speak in the morning   fragile   we hear the pans clink
each bead of my necklace   as when a heart drops a beat
letters pulled from the box   any child's ball kicked
against the wall   your glasses ponderous   some
would say old   selfish like eating like fornication   this too
taking out the garbage on a mooncold night
the furnace kicking on   even the fighting   frustrated to tears
an infant learning colors by taste   wooden steps to the front porch
the doorknob turning   late sadness   a cathedral   the soaked-in-color
glass like the smallest flowers   deeps extracted   from mere petals

Lake Louise

The water is green, glacial green, opaque
beneath the red hulls of canoes.
Horses step through the silted shallows, their riders
too young not to trust them. Once into woods,
we find the elusive shooting star in profusion
near water-streaked rocks, pointing its small beak
downward. Serrated leaves of wild strawberry.

The path leads to a tea house. Other paths disappear beyond.
Here, a woman digs a hole with a teaspoon and slips
a cluster of seeds into soil to celebrate a wedding.
Another lets her husband's ashes silt
onto the surface of the river—and as we descend,
at every creek crossing, every waterfall, we greet him,
"Dave!!" (Although we never knew him.)

The first woman, who lives on the road, confesses
that she carries her dog's ashes in her suitcase
because the dog did not like to be left behind.
She can't lock her in storage, won't ask friends
to set her on a mantel.
                              Dave, the husband,
loved to travel, and he, too, has been passengered
to Peru, Salt Lake City, Limoges.

We had been scanning the glacier for cracks
in the snow banks, and at the moment—this is true—
when Dave was tapped from his glass vial, the snow broke
above the cliffs, thundered, avalanched:
all powdery, billowy.

We descended, talking in pairs, falling back,
reassembling, talking, taking photos of the landscape
we couldn't possibly hold inside a lens. We walked
through spongy forest with yellow-green growth
rocketing out the ends of the pine boughs, past cliffs
softened by bluebells, past strange grey flats,
channels where water formerly ran.

A girl with a tiny pink backpack trailed her parents,
picking her way along the path beside us,
stone to stone. "What are you doing?" we asked.
"Oh," she said, not looking up, sighting the next rock,
"Trying not to touch the ground."

—for Reiko Yamada and Susan Goethel Campbell

I will die

in bed, reading, bundled in down,
the smooth stone of my lover's body
beside me, her book marked and laid
on the nightstand, glasses folded.
I slip away like the children in books,
squeezing under a trapdoor, stepping
through a wardrobe or skipping
across a magic bridge. The duke
and duchess invite the children
for tea, make them believe
they are royalty. Will I choose
to stay in this book?—
Although I love the secret place
the parents don't know, the tinkling
of the duchess's sleigh, the neigh
of horses in the snow, I'll step
through the cover, back
to our bed, because I want
the feel of another book,
a different cover in my hands,
slick library cellophane, bent
paperback or rough-to-the-touch
red cloth. I want more nights
with my lover, reading her
to sleep. I want her
to read to me while I cook,
her tuneful voice,
and the onions sizzling
in the pan.

Squirrel with an Apple

Sitting on its haunches, its back curved, a human-like pose,
it held a green apple and ate, its mouth moving fast as a machine—
so fast I thought it must be an illusion of the flickering leaves—
its mouth in furious, impersonal motion. It looked at me as its teeth ticked
and rotated the apple slowly in its paws. I wanted to be more interested
than I was, wished for a naturalist's curiosity—then felt consigned
to be myself. It's hard to know when to push to improve,
and when to simply say, *this is what I am*. I am the luckiest
in the world—born into stability, a genteel poverty that grew
quickly into enough. I have wine with dinner. I am well loved,
well employed. And no, this is not moving toward a *but*,
a lyric emptiness. I have been reading Larry Levis this morning.
I know that way: the poem that always swerves toward loneliness.
One of my students wishes I were her mother. She was hurt, tortured:
scalding baths, ground glass in the applesauce. But I can't
be her mother. When the painter makes a mistake, something unsightly,
she says the remedy is to continue. To fill the hole the mother made
is a life-long, impossible task. I say this as if I knew something.
I've only learned to trust my body, which says *sleep, sleep, sleep some more*.
Says *touch*. Yellow-orange squash blossoms and the fat green
of the leaves. If there's any cure, it is color, on the slab of paper,
or sown into dirt, the sky before dark when it arrays itself
in gauzy grays, and orange traces the underside of clouds. See,
this is not longing. A deep quiet rises sometimes, when I wait
in line at the grocery, the movies. Something I can rest in,
all opinions set aside, as if they could dissolve. They don't.
They will be back. But this is real, an almost-sleepy peace,
my back straight, hands slack, among the breathing others.

Shadows, Saddle Canyon

The sand's loose. The river, careless.

After the last of the shifting fire,
they show sudden on the cliff, pitched
by the moon's illumination,
each a bud-sheath, hood and stem:
a procession of humped gods
ancient as breathing.

I'm altered by these shapes.
The current moves, taking, embracing.
For once, I'm unafraid.

The shadows, great and still, still unfold. I swell
toward spirit, then fall to what I am, less
than a minnow in the river's tail.

Biographical Note

Jane Hilberry's previous collection, *Body Painting*, won the Colorado Book Award for Poetry. With her father Conrad Hilberry, she co-authored *This Awkward Art: Poems by a Father and Daughter*, introduced by Richard Wilbur. Her interest in visual art led her to edit a letterpress volume titled *The Burden of the Beholder. Dave Armstrong and the Art of Collage* and to write a book of biography/art criticism called *The Erotic Art of Edgar Britton*. She also co-authored, with Mary Lynn Pulley, a little book about email, *Get Smart: How Email Can Make or Break Your Career—and Your Organization*. In addition to teaching Creative Writing, Creativity, and Literature at Colorado College, she has facilitated creativity workshops and arts-based leadership development programs across the United States and at The Banff Centre in Canada.